W9-ACR-386

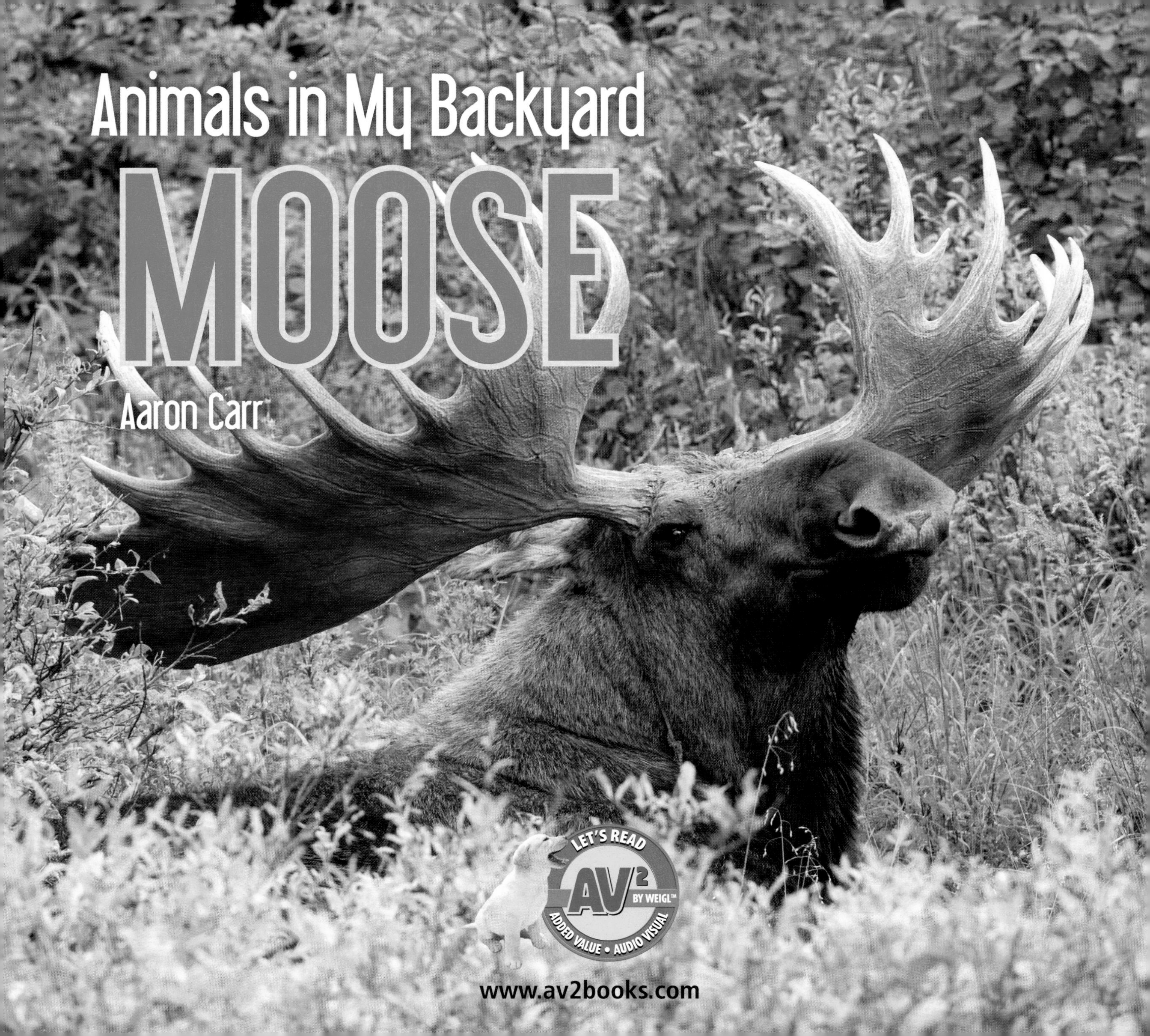
Animals in My Backyard
MOOSE
Aaron Carr
LET'S READ
AV2
BY WEIGL™
ADDED VALUE • AUDIO VISUAL
www.av2books.com

Go to **www.av2books.com**, and enter this book's unique code.

BOOK CODE

W998006

AV^2 by Weigl brings you media enhanced books that support active learning.

AV^2 provides enriched content that supplements and complements this book. Weigl's AV^2 books strive to create inspired learning and engage young minds in a total learning experience.

Your AV^2 Media Enhanced books come alive with...

Audio
Listen to sections of the book read aloud.

Video
Watch informative video clips.

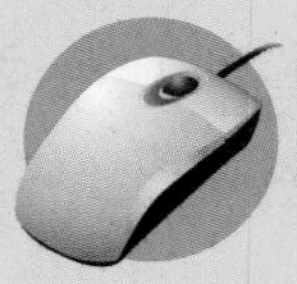

Embedded Weblinks
Gain additional information for research.

Try This!
Complete activities and hands-on experiments.

Key Words
Study vocabulary, and complete a matching word activity.

Quizzes
Test your knowledge.

Slide Show
View images and captions, and prepare a presentation.

... and much, much more!

Published by AV^2 by Weigl.
350 5th Avenue, 59th Floor New York, NY 10118
Website: www.av2books.com www.weigl.com

Library of Congress Cataloguing in Publication data available upon request.
Fax 1-866-449-3445 for the attention of the Publishing Records department.

ISBN 978-1-62127-212-0 (hardcover)
ISBN 978-1-62127-216-8 (soft cover)

Printed in the United States of America in North Mankato, Minnesota
1 2 3 4 5 6 7 8 9 0 16 15 14 13 12

122012
WEP301112

Senior Editor: Aaron Carr Art Director: Terry Paulhus

Weigl acknowledges Getty Images as the primary image supplier for this title.

Animals in My Backyard

MOOSE

CONTENTS

Meet the moose.

He looks like a very big deer.

He lives with his mother
when he is young.

When he is young,
his fur is light brown.

He has very large antlers
on his head.

On his head, his antlers
can stretch 6 feet wide.

He has a big upper lip.

His big upper lip hangs down to his chin.

He eats with his large mouth.

With his large mouth, he eats twigs, bark, grass, and other plants.

He has very long legs.

With his very long legs, he can run up to 35 miles per hour.

He has very big hoofs.

With his very big hoofs,
he can walk through snow.

He lives in the forest.

In the forest, he can find
all of the things he needs to live.

If you meet the moose,
he may be surprised.
He might run at you.

If you meet the moose,
stay away.

MOOSE FACTS

These pages provide more detail about the interesting facts found in the book. They are intended to be used by adults as a learning support to help young readers round out their knowledge of each animal featured in the *Animals in My Backyard* series.

Pages 4–5

The moose looks like a large deer. Moose are the largest members of the deer family. At the shoulder, it is taller than the largest breed of saddle horse. The largest moose live in Alaska and Siberia. They can be up to 7 feet (2 meters) tall and weigh more than 1,300 pounds (600 kilograms). Male moose, or bulls, are larger than females, or cows.

Pages 6–7

Moose live with their mothers when they are young. Moose mate in September, and their calves are born around June. Mothers carry their babies for 230 days before giving birth to one or two calves. Newborn calves are tan in color and weigh about 30 pounds (14 kg). Calves stay with their mother for one year before going to live on their own.

Pages 8–9

Moose have very large antlers. Only male moose grow antlers. They begin growing antlers each summer. Moose antlers can stretch more than 6 feet (1.8 m) from end to end and weigh up to 70 pounds (20 kg). Antlers are full-grown by late August or early September. They may have up to 30 tines, or spikes. Moose use their antlers to defend themselves from predators. They shed their antlers in November.

Pages 10–11

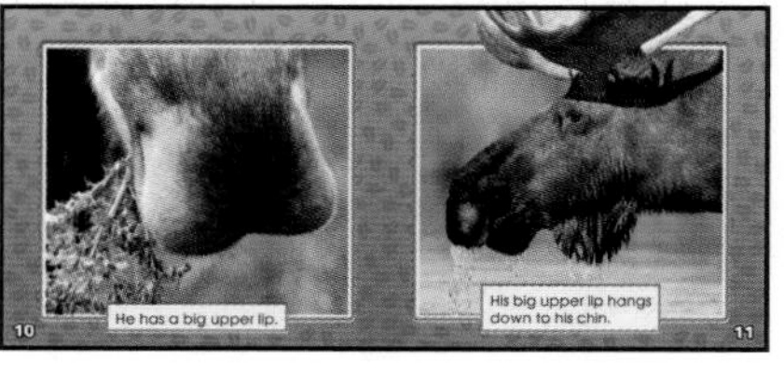

The moose has a large upper lip. Its muzzle hangs down over its chin. The muzzle sways like a pendulum when the moose moves. Scientists believe the moose's muzzle adapted to allow it to eat plants from the bottoms of lakes and rivers. Moose can dive more than 20 feet (5.5 m) under water to search for food. They can stay under for up to 50 seconds.

Pages 12–13

Moose eat plants. The moose was named for the Algonquin First Nation word *mooswa*, which means "twig-eater." In the summer, moose eat twigs, tree bark, many kinds of grasses, leaves, and a variety of aquatic plants. During winter, moose mostly eat pine cones and shrubs. They also use their hoofs to scrape away snow so they can eat mosses and lichens.

Pages 14–15

Moose have very long legs. They can sometimes have gray or white coloring on their legs, called stockings. Though moose look large and awkward, they can move quite well, both on land and in water. Moose can sprint up to 35 miles (56 km) per hour, and they can trot at a steady speed of 20 miles (32 km) per hour for one hour. Moose can swim more than 10 miles (16 km).

Pages 16–17

Moose have very big hoofs. The moose's hoofs can be up to 7 inches (18 centimeters) across. These hoofs are cloven, or divided. This allows the hoofs to spread out and cover a larger area. Moose use their large hoofs like snowshoes. Their large hoofs let the moose walk more easily in both snow and mud.

Pages 18–19

Moose live in the forest. They inhabit the boreal forests of North America, Europe, and Asia. In North America, they are also found in the western mountain regions and in the northern tundra of Alaska. Moose have traditionally stayed in cold northern climates that are home to the kinds of food and shelter they prefer. In recent years, however, moose have been spotted farther south.

Pages 20–21

If you meet the moose, stay away. Moose usually live by themselves in remote forest areas. However, people still come into contact with moose in nature. When this happens, it is important to keep your distance from the moose. Moose can be bold, and they have been known to charge at people to defend themselves.

KEY WORDS

Research has shown that as much as 65 percent of all written material published in English is made up of 300 words. These 300 words cannot be taught using pictures or learned by sounding them out. They must be recognized by sight. This book contains 46 common sight words to help young readers improve their reading fluency and comprehension. This book also teaches young readers several important content words. These words are paired with pictures to aid in learning and improve understanding.

Page	Sight Words First Appearance
4	the
5	a, big, he, like, looks, very
6	his, is, light, lives, mother, when, with, young
8	has, head, large, on
9	can, feet
11	down, to
12	eats
13	and, other, plants
14	long
15	miles, run, up
16	through, walk
18	in
19	all, find, needs, of, things
20	at, away, be, if, may, might, you

Page	Content Words First Appearance
4	moose
5	deer
6	fur
8	antlers
10	lip
11	chin
12	mouth
13	bark, grass, twigs
14	legs
15	hour
16	hoofs, snow
18	forest

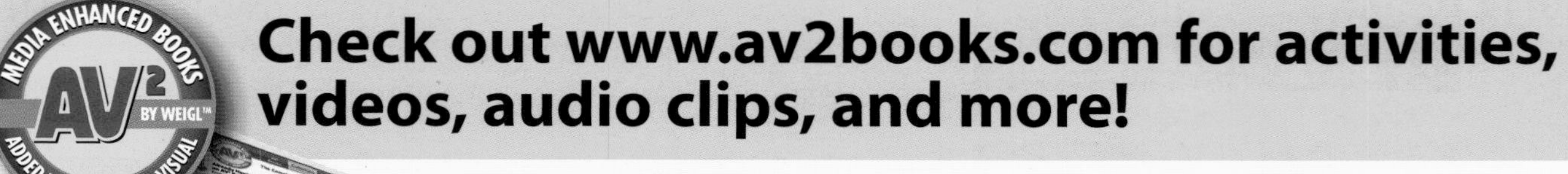

3 Fuel your imagination online!

www.av2books.com